THE ENVIRONMENT DETECTIVE INVESTIGATES

Making Air Cleaner

Jen Green

WAYLAND

First published in 2010 by Wayland
Copyright © Wayland 2010

Wayland
Hachette Children's Books
338 Euston Road
London NW1 3BH

Wayland Australia
Level 17/207 Kent Street
Sydney NSW 2000

Editor: Katie Powell
Designer: Stephen Prosser
Maps and artwork: Peter Bull Art Studio
Sherlock Bones artwork: Richard Hook
Picture Researcher: Shelley Noronha
Consultant: Michael Scott, OBE

British Library Cataloguing in Publication Data
Green, Jen.
    Making air cleaner. -- (The environment detective
    investigates)
    1. Air quality management--Juvenile literature. 2. Air--
    Pollution--Juvenile literature.
    I. Title II. Series
    363.7'3926-dc22

ISBN: 978 0 7502 6258 3

Printed in China

Printed in China

Wayland is a division of Hachette Children's Books,
an Hachette UK Company,
www.hachette.co.uk.

Picture acknowledgements:
The author and publisher would like to thank the
following for allowing their pictures to be reproduced
in this book: cover © Purcell-Holmes/Robert, title page
© Bob Sacha/Corbis, imprint page © Gary
Braasch/Corbis, 4 © Wayland, 5 © iStock, 6 ©
Wayland, 7 © Gary Braasch/Corbis, 8 © Hulton
Archive/Getty Images, 9 © Kentaroo Tryman/Getty
Images, 10 © iStock, 11 © Wayland, 12 ©
Wayland, 13 © Bob Sacha/Corbis, 14 © Wayland,
15 © iStock, 16 © NASA, 17 © iStock, 18 © Echo/
Getty Images, 19 © Still Pictures, 20 © Wayland,
21 © iStock, 22 © Ian Waldie/Getty Images, 23 ©
AFP/Getty Images, 24 © Samuel Aranda/Getty Images,
25 © iStock, 26 © Paul Burns/Getty Images, 27 ©
iStock, 28 © iStock, 29 © iStock

Contents

Words that appear in **bold** can be
found in the glossary on page 30.

🐾 The Environment Detective, Sherlock Bones, will help you learn about
air pollution and ways to make the air cleaner. The answers to Sherlock's
questions appear on page 31.

Why is clean air important?

Earth's **atmosphere** is a layer of gases surrounding the planet. The atmosphere contains a mixture of gases we call the air. All living things need air, and humans can't survive for much more than a few minutes without it. Without air, the Earth would be as hostile and lifeless as the Moon.

The atmosphere surrounds our planet like the rind on an apple. It extends about 1,000 kilometres into space. Earth's **gravity** holds the gases in place. Because of gravity, the air just above the planet surface contains most gases. The gases thin out as you move towards space. The atmosphere protects us from harmful **solar** radiation. Rocks and dust from space, called **meteors**, mostly burn up in the atmosphere instead of falling to Earth.

ECO-FACTS

What is air pollution?

Pollution is any substance that harms the natural world. Pollution can affect the air, water or soil. Air pollution includes smoke from a cigarette, exhaust fumes from a truck and soot from a factory chimney. Some types of pollution make the air dirty or smelly, but other types cannot be seen or smelled.

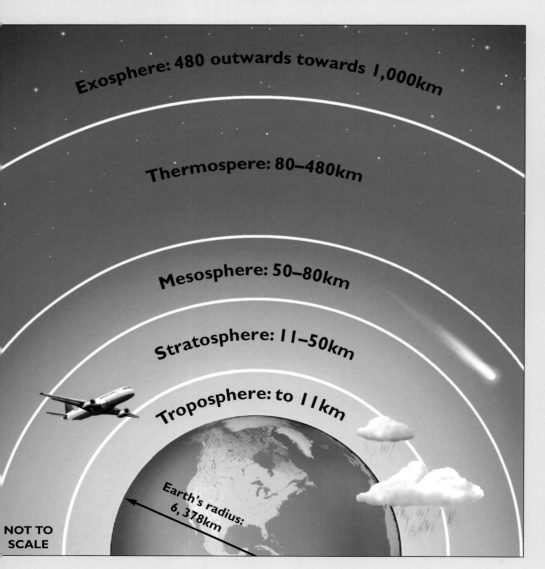

Exosphere: 480 outwards towards 1,000km

Thermospere: 80–480km

Mesosphere: 50–80km

Stratosphere: 11–50km

Troposphere: to 11km

Earth's radius: 6,378km

NOT TO SCALE

Scientists distinguish five layers in the atmosphere. Clouds and storms form in the lowest layer, the troposphere. Aircraft fly in the calm layer above. Meteors burn up in the mesosphere, causing 'shooting stars'.

🐾 **In which layer of the atmosphere do aircraft fly?**

Smoke, soot and carbon dioxide gas are given off when wood or coal is burned.

Air is mostly made up of two gases: nitrogen (78 per cent) and **oxygen** (nearly 21 per cent). The remaining 1 per cent is mostly argon (0.93 per cent) with small amounts of **hydrogen**, **carbon dioxide** (CO_2), methane and other gases. Air also contains floating **particles** of pollen, dust, salt and **water vapour**. Clean air has no colour or scent.

Clean air is vital to life on Earth, but nowadays people are producing air pollution, which is harming wildlife and our own health, and even affecting the climate. As human populations grow and industries develop, so the problem is getting worse. This book will explain the causes of air pollution and how we can all help to keep the air clean and healthy.

DETECTIVE WORK

You can test for pollution in the local air by looking at **lichen**. These are plant-like growths found on rocks and buildings. Tall, hairy lichens that resemble miniature shrubs only grow in clean air. Flat lichens grow in more polluted air.

How is the air kept clean naturally?

The balance of gases in the air is maintained by natural cycles. Thanks to these cycles, the mixture of gases in the air has remained about the same for thousands of years.

Plants and animals help to maintain the natural balance of oxygen and carbon dioxide in the air. Plants use carbon dioxide to live and grow. They convert carbon dioxide, water and minerals into plant food using sunlight energy. This process releases oxygen. Animals breathe in oxygen and give out carbon dioxide (**respiration**). Forests act as giant stores of carbon which is released when wood is burned. The oceans and soil also store carbon dioxide.

DETECTIVE WORK

As fuels burn they use up oxygen. To test this, light a candle and put a jar over it. When the oxygen in the jar is used up, the candle will go out.

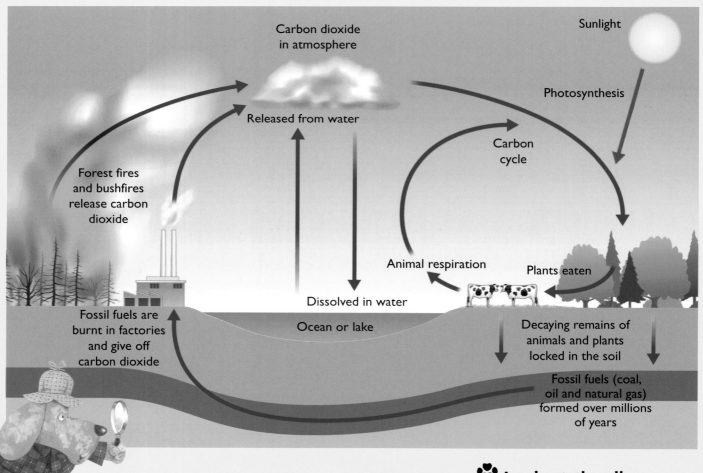

Carbon dioxide in atmosphere

Sunlight

Photosynthesis

Released from water

Forest fires and bushfires release carbon dioxide

Carbon cycle

Animal respiration

Plants eaten

Dissolved in water

Fossil fuels are burnt in factories and give off carbon dioxide

Ocean or lake

Decaying remains of animals and plants locked in the soil

Fossil fuels (coal, oil and natural gas) formed over millions of years

This diagram shows the carbon cycle. Carbon stored in plants and the bodies of animals is released when they die and rot.

Look at the diagram. Name the processes which release carbon dioxide.

When a volcano erupts, huge quantities of ash, steam and gas shoot high in the air. Mount St Helens in western United States, erupted in 1985.

Carbon dioxide, methane and other gases high in the atmosphere allow sunlight through, but then trap some of the Sun's heat and stop it escaping back into space. They act like the glass in a greenhouse, keeping the air and land below at comfortable temperatures for living things. This is called the **Greenhouse Effect** and the gases are called **greenhouse gases**. The Sun heats the air in different parts of the planet unevenly. This sets air moving, producing winds. Winds help to spread the Sun's warmth around the Earth. They can also spread pollution, and eventually disperse it.

Not all pollution is man-made. Air pollution happens naturally when dust is lifted and carried by the wind, or when smoky forest fires are sparked by lightning. Volcanic eruptions can shoot a huge plume of ash high into the atmosphere. The ash partly blocks sunlight, which makes temperatures cooler. Eventually winds disperse the ash, or it falls to Earth.

ECO-FACTS

Death of the dinosaurs

Most scientists believe dinosaurs died out 65 million years ago because of a disaster which triggered severe air pollution. The pollution may have been caused by a massive volcanic eruption or by a giant rock from space hitting the Earth. The impact would have raised a huge dust cloud which blotted out sunlight, so plants could not grow. Dinosaurs died out when plant food became scarce.

How do people cause air pollution?

In the last 200 years, man-made pollution has started to affect the balance of gases in the air. Factories and power stations pollute the air as they burn **fuels** for energy or process **raw materials**. From the late 1700s, human activities began to produce serious air pollution.

People have been producing small amounts of pollution ever since prehistoric times, when humans learned to make fire, and started to burn wood for heating and cooking. Later, coal was burned as fuel. In the late 1700s, the steam engine was invented. Coal was burned to turn water to steam, which was used to drive machinery. Factories opened all over Europe and North America. This was the start of the Industrial Revolution – and the start of serious air pollution.

ECO-FACTS

Smog from coal
By the early 1900s, coal was the main fuel burned in homes in cities. However, burning coal releases smoke and soot. This pollution combined with fog to produce a poisonous haze called **smog**. In 1952, smog killed 4,000 people in London. Coal fires were banned and people had to use new 'smokeless fuels' instead. The new fuels still released pollution but produced less harmful soot.

The London smogs of the 1950s were so thick they were known as 'pea-soupers'.

Coal, oil and natural gas are now our main source of energy. These fuels are called **fossil fuels** because they are the fossilised remains of prehistoric forests (coal) and tiny sea creatures (oil and gas). Fossil fuels are burned in power stations to **generate** electricity. Burning fossil fuels is a major cause of air pollution. Power stations and factories release smoke, soot, carbon dioxide and other harmful gases, such as sulphur dioxide and nitrogen oxides.

Not all power stations burn fossil fuels. Nuclear plants process a mineral called uranium to release heat and energy. This process does not give off carbon dioxide, but it does produce very dangerous **radioactive** waste. Accidents at nuclear power plants such as Chernobyl in Ukraine in 1986, have caused very harmful air pollution.

Nuclear power plants don't give off smoke and soot but they can still produce highly dangerous radioactive waste.

DETECTIVE WORK

In the 1950s and 60s, smog killed hundreds of people in New York City. Find out more about this or about the London 'pea-soupers' using a library or the Internet.

How does transport cause air pollution?

Along with factories and power stations, cars, trucks, trains and planes are a major source of air pollution. Aircraft release a lot of pollution high in the atmosphere. As well as carbon dioxide, vehicles produce harmful fumes as they burn fuels such as petrol, diesel and **kerosene**.

Fumes from car exhausts build up when streets are clogged in rush hours.

Petrol, diesel and kerosene are made from oil. When burned they give off carbon monoxide, sulphur dioxide and nitrogen oxides. These waste gases can all cause health problems. Carbon monoxide can give you a headache or make you sleepy. Sulphur dioxide and nitrogen oxides can cause breathing problems, while soot from diesel can cause cancer. Devices called **catalytic converters** (cat) can be fitted to cars to reduce pollution, and new models of car are often 'cleaner'. However, every week there are thousands of new cars on the roads, which add to the pollution.

DETECTIVE WORK

Investigate pollution given off by cars with the help of an adult. Tie a small cotton cloth over a cold exhaust pipe, and secure it with a rubber band. Ask the adult to run the car engine for two minutes, and then when the pipe is cool, to carefully remove the cloth. The soot found on the cloth usually ends up in the air.

Lead used to be added to petrol to make engines run efficiently. Then, scientists discovered that lead fumes are poisonous. Lead can cause brain damage in young children. The risk is greatest for people living on busy roads. Now most petrol is lead-free. In the United States, a ban on leaded petrol led to a 98 per cent reduction in lead pollution.

Waste gases from cars and factories react with sunlight in hot countries to form a type of smog called **photochemical smog**. This brown, dirty haze particularly affects cities that lie in valleys surrounded by mountains, such as Los Angeles in western United States, and Mexico City. The smog causes breathing problems. In sunny weather when the smog is bad, some people wear a mask when they go outdoors.

ECO-FACTS

Catalytic converter

A catalytic converter is a box that fits onto the car exhaust. It works as a filter, converting poisonous gases into less harmful ones. But the new gases still cause pollution. In addition, the cat only works properly when it gets hot, so it does not filter effectively on short journeys.

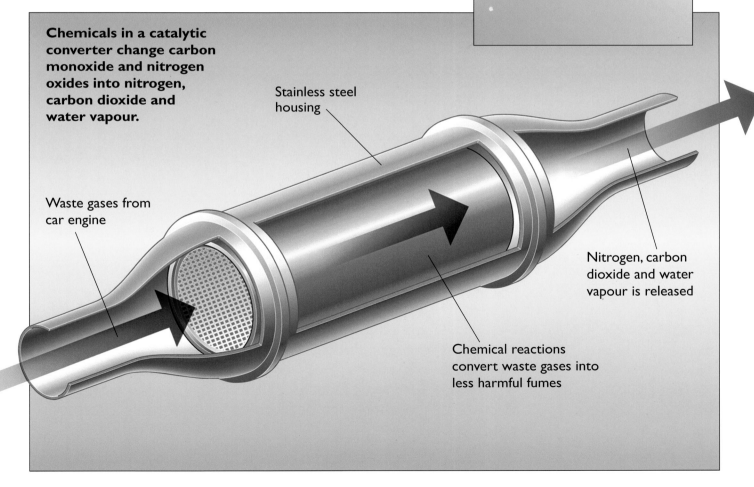

Chemicals in a catalytic converter change carbon monoxide and nitrogen oxides into nitrogen, carbon dioxide and water vapour.

Stainless steel housing

Waste gases from car engine

Nitrogen, carbon dioxide and water vapour is released

Chemical reactions convert waste gases into less harmful fumes

Which countries produce air pollution?

Across the world, some countries produce more pollution than others. However, air pollution from cars, factories and power stations spreads on the wind to affect remote areas. Scientists have even found traces of pollution in Antarctica, where there are no factories or towns.

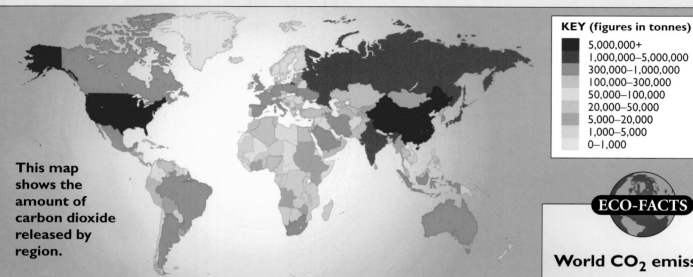

This map shows the amount of carbon dioxide released by region.

KEY (figures in tonnes)

5,000,000+
1,000,000–5,000,000
300,000–1,000,000
100,000–300,000
50,000–100,000
20,000–50,000
5,000–20,000
1,000–5,000
0–1,000

More developed countries in North America, Europe and the Middle East produce far more air pollution per person than less developed regions such as Africa. This is because there are more factories and power stations, and people have cars, computers, televisions, fridges, cookers and other machines that use energy. On the plus side, more developed countries often have strict anti-pollution laws, and the money to spend on technology that reduces pollution.

Countries	Total amount of CO_2 released in 2006 (tonnes)
China	6,103,493
India	1,510,351
Italy	474,148
Canada	544,680
Japan	1,293,409
Germany	805,090
United Kingdom	568,520
South Korea	475,248
Russia	1,564,669
United States	5,752,289

🐾 **What country ranks third in the world in total carbon emissions, but only 16th in the amount released per person?**

ECO-FACTS

World CO_2 emissions

Look at the table on the left. China is the biggest CO_2 producer, releasing 21.5 per cent of **emissions**. Next is the United States of America (20 per cent), Russia (5.5 per cent) and India (5.3 per cent). But China and India have large populations, so the amount of CO_2 produced per person is low. The United States ranks fifth in the world in terms of CO_2 released per person. Russia ranks 16th, China 80th and India 116th out of 176 countries.

Less developed regions, such as Africa, produce far less pollution per person, because there are fewer factories and machines, so energy needs are lower. However, the populations of many developing countries are rising fast, and as their industries develop, so they are producing more pollution. For example, China is building many new power plants to meet its energy needs. Some, but not all, developing countries have strict anti-pollution laws. 'Clean' technology such as lead-free petrol is more expensive, so some developing countries cannot afford it. The air in many cities in the developing world still contains high levels of lead.

Some big businesses are multi-national operations with factories in many countries. In the 1980s, the American chemicals manufacturer Union Carbide owned a chemicals factory in Bhopal, India. In 1984, five tonnes of poisonous gas leaked from the plant, killing 6,500 people and injuring thousands more. Twenty-five years on, the area around the factory, devastated and closed by the disaster, is still polluted.

China's energy needs are expanding as its industries develop. In 2007, it built at least one new power plant every week.

DETECTIVE WORK

Find out more about the amount of pollution produced by country by logging onto: www.nationmaster.com/index.php and selecting Environment. How much pollution does the United Kingdom produce?

What makes air acidic?

Some types of air pollution only harm the local area. Other kinds can be carried long distances to affect people and places hundreds of kilometres away. **Acid rain** is an example of air pollution that can carry a long way.

Acid rain is caused by waste gases given off by factories, cars and coal-fired power stations. When sulphur dioxide and nitrogen oxides mix with water vapour in the air, they form weak acids. The moisture drifts and eventually condenses to form clouds which shed acid rain, sleet or snow. When the weak acid is taken up by tree roots, leaves wither and the tree may eventually die. The acid also ends up in lakes where it can kill fish such as salmon. Acid rain can even eat into stone, affecting buildings in cities.

🐾 **Look at the diagram below. Is acid rain only caused by man-made pollution, or are there any natural causes?**

ECO-FACTS

Transboundary pollution

Waste gases released by industries in one country can drift across national borders before falling as acid rain in another country. This is called **transboundary** pollution. Thousands of lakes in Scandinavia have been contaminated by pollution from the United Kingdom and Germany. Canadian forests have been harmed by waste gases from the United States of America.

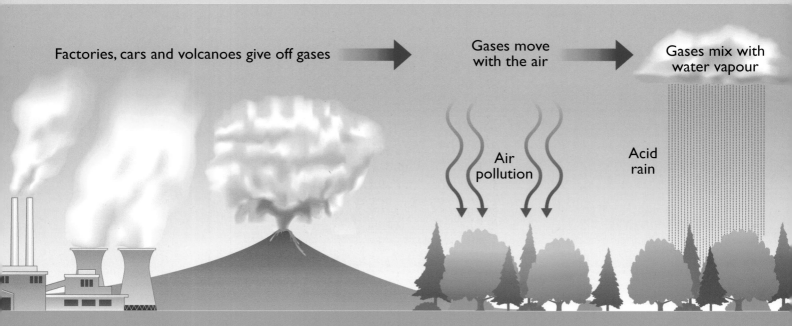

Factories, cars and volcanoes give off gases

Gases move with the air

Gases mix with water vapour

Air pollution

Acid rain

This artwork shows how acid rain is caused by air pollution.

**These trees in Poland have been killed by acid rain.
Do trees in your area show signs of damage?**

Scientists have found several ways of tackling acid rain.
Quantities of lime can be dumped on lakes to neutralise the
acid. This has been done in Sweden, but only provides a
temporary solution. Factories and power plants can be built
with taller chimneys, but this only delivers the pollution to
higher levels in the atmosphere. Devices called **scrubbers** can
be fitted to factory chimneys to filter the waste gases, but this
is expensive. As more countries become **industrialised**, so
more areas are being affected by acid rain. The real solution
is to use cleaner fuels such as natural gas or wind or solar
energy. Since cars also contribute to acid rain, the problem
can be eased by using cars less and public transport more.

DETECTIVE WORK

Test the effects of acid
rain by putting water
mixed with vinegar
(a weak acid) into a jar.
Dip a few leaves in the
mixture and leave them
with their stalks in the
vinegar. They will soon
turn brown. Look for
similar damage to trees
in your neighbourhood.

What new chemicals cause air pollution?

Man-made chemicals can be very useful. In the twentieth century, the development of new chemicals improved efficiency in industry, manufacturing and farming. However, a few chemicals were discovered to produce harmful pollution.

In the 1980s, scientists discovered that something was harming a layer of a gas called ozone, which occurs naturally in the stratosphere. The **ozone layer** acts as a shield, filtering out harmful **ultraviolet rays** in sunlight, which can cause skin cancer and eye damage. But now the ozone layer was becoming thinner. The damage was traced to chemicals called **chlorofluorocarbons (CFCs)**, used in the manufacture of fridges and aerosol sprays. At a conference in Canada in 1987, most nations agreed to stop using CFCs. However the chemicals linger for many years, so the ozone layer will not recover until at least 2050. Ozone loss means it's especially important to wear sun cream to protect your skin from the sun.

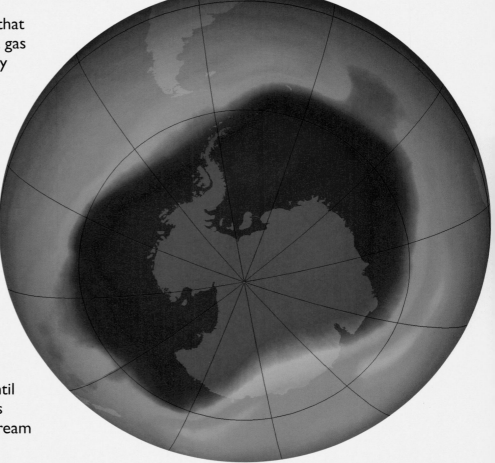

This picture taken by satellite shows the ozone 'hole' over Antarctica in 2006. During the 1980s and 90s, ozone loss increased, and this hole got bigger.

DETECTIVE WORK

Sun creams of different strengths are available in chemists. Creams rated factor 15 and over offer high protection. Thirty years ago, factor 15 was about the highest protection available, but now higher factors are recommended. What is the highest factor on sale in chemists today?

ECO-FACTS

Silent Spring

In the 1950s and 1960s, a powerful insecticide called DDT was widely used in farming. But a US scientist, Rachel Carson, wrote a book called *Silent Spring*, which warned that the pesticide was killing songbirds. If all songbirds died, springs would become silent. Partly thanks to *Silent Spring*, DDT was banned in the United States in the 1970s, and in much of Europe in the 1980s. However, it is still widely used in other parts of the world.

In recent years, scientists have discovered that chemicals called Persistent Organic Pollutants (POPs) can leak into the air to harm people and wildlife. POPs include metals used in industry and also **insecticides**, which farmers spray on crops to kill insect pests. On farmland, the poison is absorbed by crop-eating mice and insects. It then passes to predators such as birds, that eat mice or insects. In this way, it spreads through the natural world. **Conservation** groups helped to spread the word about POPs. Some more developed countries have now banned them, but they are still used in the developing world.

DDT is still widely used to spray crops in India and many less developed countries. The spray can drift in the wind, too.

What causes indoor pollution?

The air inside homes, schools and other buildings can be polluted as well as the air outdoors. This is becoming more important as both adults and young people spend more time indoors.

Some indoor air pollution comes from natural causes. Pollen, animal hair and dust may all make you sneeze or give you asthma. Man-made chemicals called volatile organic compounds (VOCs for short) also cause health problems. These are found in products we use at home, including paints, glues, aerosol sprays and cleaning products. Like dust and pollen, VOCs can cause asthma and allergies. They can also give you a headache or make you feel sick and dizzy. Scientists have discovered that high levels of VOCs are quite common in homes, especially ones with double glazing, which keeps in heat – and also pollution.

ECO-FACTS

Germs and infection

Viruses and bacteria are microscopic living things that cause many kinds of illness, including 'flu and the common cold. Often simply called 'germs', they are spread through the air by coughing and sneezing. Always use a tissue or cover your mouth when you sneeze or cough to avoid spreading infection.

Nowadays many young people suffer from breathing problems and have to use an inhaler. Asthma can be caused by indoor or outdoor pollution.

✿ Name three everyday products found in homes that may contain VOCs.

Smoking is a major cause of indoor pollution. Cigarette smoke contains harmful carbon monoxide, nicotine and tar. It can cause serious diseases such as heart disease and lung cancer. Unfortunately, smoking can harm not only the smoker but other people in the room – this is called passive smoking. Smoking is particularly dangerous because it is addictive – once you start, it's difficult to stop. Smoking is also really expensive, so the best thing is never to start.

Many types of indoor pollution can be solved fairly easily, by removing the source of pollution. For example, paints and cleaning products containing high levels of VOCs have to be clearly labelled. Encourage your family to choose brands or types that are more **environmentally-friendly**. Simply opening a window to let in fresh air will reduce indoor pollution. Always open a window if you are using glue or oil-based paint.

If you are in a room where people are smoking, you breathe in smoke, too. In many countries, smoking is now banned in public places such as cinemas, restaurants and bars.

DETECTIVE WORK

Carry out a survey among your friends and family to find out how many people suffer from asthma or allergies. Record the results by age, under these headings: Under 15s, 15–30s, Over 30s. Which age group is most affected?

How is air pollution affecting Earth's climate?

Natural levels of greenhouse gases in the atmosphere keep Earth at a comfortable temperature for living things. Now, however, human activities are increasing levels of greenhouse gases, which is causing **climate change**.

Carbon dioxide is the main greenhouse gas, released when fossil fuels are burned. All over the world, factories, power stations and vehicles are releasing it. Methane, nitrous oxide and CFCs are also greenhouse gases. Methane is given off by swamps, rubbish dumps, rice-fields and animals such as cattle. All of these gases are acting to trap more of the Sun's heat in the atmosphere, which is making the Earth heat up. This is called **global warming**.

ECO-FACTS

Natural climate change

Some climate change happens naturally. In Earth's long history, the climate has warmed and cooled many times. Long, cold periods called **Ice Ages** are separated by warmer periods. The Earth has been slowly warming since the last Ice Age ended 10,000 years ago. However, scientists are convinced that human activities are greatly increasing the speed and scale of global warming.

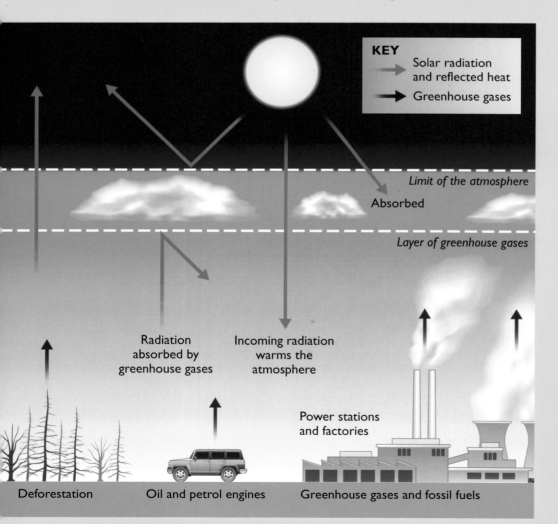

KEY
→ Solar radiation and reflected heat
→ Greenhouse gases

Limit of the atmosphere

Absorbed

Layer of greenhouse gases

Radiation absorbed by greenhouse gases

Incoming radiation warms the atmosphere

Power stations and factories

Deforestation

Oil and petrol engines

Greenhouse gases and fossil fuels

Natural greenhouse gases in the atmosphere act like the glass in a greenhouse, trapping reflected heat from the Sun. Now, human activities are adding more greenhouse gases.

Levels of carbon dioxide in the air are now a third higher than they were at the start of the Industrial Revolution. Scientists believe that four-fifths of this comes from burning fossil fuels. The rest comes from burning forests. Since the 1900s, about 30 per cent of the world's forests have been cleared for farming. When forests are cleared, the wood is mostly burned, which releases stored carbon. Furthermore, once the forests are gone, they no longer absorb carbon dioxide and release oxygen. So forest clearance has a double impact on the environment.

Since 1900, average temperatures have risen 0.5°C. Glaciers and ice in the polar regions have started to melt, adding water to the oceans. The greater volume of water is making sea levels rise. The oceans are also expanding because of warmer temperatures – and releasing more carbon dioxide. If this trend continues, low-lying areas such as Bangladesh in southern Asia, and the Maldives in the Indian Ocean, could be at risk of flooding.

Since the 1980s, every decade has been warmer than the decade before. As a result, the polar ice caps are starting to melt.

DETECTIVE WORK

Test the greenhouse effect using two jars of water. Put one jar outdoors in the sun and the other behind glass, such as in a greenhouse or on a sunny windowsill. Use a thermometer to take the water temperature after an hour. How do the two jars compare?

How will climate change affect the planet?

Climate change is a serious environmental problem. Scientists cannot predict exactly what the effects will be, but extreme weather may well become more common. So what can be done?

In future, rising sea levels will increase the risk of flooding on coasts and islands around the world. Low-lying countries such as Holland and Bangladesh, in southern Asia, could be badly affected. One-fifth of the world's population lives near the coast. Wildlife will also be affected. As **habitats** become warmer, some animals and plants will struggle to survive.

DETECTIVE WORK
Ask your teacher if you can have a class discussion about the causes and effects of climate change, and what can be done about it.

Forest fires often start during **droughts**. In 2001, a large bushfire threatened to destroy homes in Sydney, Australia.

🐾 **How do bushfires harm the environment?**

Scientists use powerful computers to predict the effects of climate change. The computers predict that weather patterns will become more changeable, and in recent years, there have been many examples of extreme weather, which seem to confirm the predictions. Dry places such as Africa and Australia have experienced droughts. Meanwhile some wet areas have experienced unusually heavy rains, which has resulted in floods. In future, areas that are now farmland could become infertile because of either drought or flooding.

We have to act now to tackle climate change. The main way is to reduce output of greenhouse gases. This means using less fossil fuels and relying more on alternative energy sources that cause less pollution. Since the 1990s, the world's nations have met at conferences to try to agree cuts in the amount of greenhouse gas each nation produces. However, it is very hard to reach agreement. At the Copenhagen Conference in 2009, nations failed to agree the cuts necessary to keep the temperature increase below 2°C.

The world's nations met to discuss climate in Copenhagen, Denmark in 2009. Many countries were reluctant to agree cuts they believed would harm their economy or prevent their industries developing.

ECO-FACTS

Carbon trading

Carbon trading is a method of counteracting the pollution caused by greenhouse gases. Countries that produce a lot of carbon dioxide pay for trees to be planted elsewhere to absorb carbon dioxide. The drawback is that newly planted trees take at least 25 years to reduce carbon dioxide and counter the effects of today's pollution.

What can be done to tackle air pollution?

In the last 20 years or so, we have discovered more about the dangers of air pollution. Scientists have made progress in tackling problems such as ozone loss. However, there is still a lot to do. Governments, conservation groups, businesses and ordinary people are all involved.

There are two main ways to tackle air pollution. First, we can clean up the effects of existing air pollution, for example by using lime to treat lakes affected by acid rain. Second, we can reduce pollution before it happens, for example by removing lead from petrol, or banning smoking in public places. Because of the difficulties of cleaning up air pollution, reducing the pollution created in the first place is often less expensive in the long-term, as well as being better for the environment.

Traffic-free shopping areas such as this one in Barcelona, Spain help to improve air quality in towns and cities.

ECO-FACTS

Reducing traffic pollution

In cities such as London and Singapore, motorists now pay a fee to enter the city centre. The money raised by the 'congestion charge' is used to improve public transport. Singapore has a very efficient train service that encourages motorists to leave their cars at home.

DETECTIVE WORK

In many countries, a ban on smoking in public places has improved air quality. However, the ban is unpopular with some smokers. Ask your friends and family what they think about smoking bans. You could record the results in two columns, for and against, and give reasons why.

How do wind and solar power help to tackle climate change?

The city of Copenhagen has an unusual public heating system. Houses are heated by hot water from shared boilers. This causes much less pollution than heating individual homes.

Factories and power stations are responsible for a lot of pollution. Many governments now require these industries to filter their waste gases, and fine companies that cause air pollution. Devices such as scrubbers (see page 15) are expensive, but companies save the money they would pay in fines. Governments are now funding research into cleaner energy sources such as wind turbines and solar power, to reduce our dependence on fossil fuels.

Planes and cars are a major source of air pollution. Many air passengers now pay a small charge to offset the pollution caused when they fly. The average family car produces 4–5 tonnes of carbon dioxide a year. Governments can encourage people to use cars less by providing efficient public transport. For example in New Dehli, India, the authorities have reduced pollution by providing a fleet of buses that run on cleaner natural gas.

How can I help to make air cleaner?

Everyone has a right to breathe clean, healthy air. Air pollution and climate change are major challenges, but they can be beaten if everyone works together. There are things we can all do to improve air quality which will benefit people, and also wildlife and the natural world.

The power stations that supply energy to our homes release harmful gases. We can reduce this pollution by using less energy. This can be done quite easily. For example, families can use low-energy lightbulbs, and make sure homes are well-**insulated**, to save energy on heating. We can switch off lights and other machines when they are not in use. With simple measures like these, the average family can prevent up to two tonnes of carbon dioxide from being released in a year – an important step in tackling pollution.

Every day, we throw away packaging such as cardboard, paper and plastic, that is used to wrap food and other goods. This waste can release air pollution whether it is dumped, burned or buried. **Recycling** packaging reduces waste and pollution. Bottles, cans, boxes and cartons can all be recycled. Recycling paper and cardboard helps to protect the forests that maintain the balance of gases in the air.

ECO-FACTS

Saving trees

Forests play a vital role in keeping the air clean. In recent years, environmental groups have saved large areas of forest, such as part of the Great Bear Rainforest in Canada, from logging. You could organise a sponsored walk or bike-ride to raise money for conservation.

Recycling helps to reduce air pollution. It also saves energy and natural resources such as timber and minerals, and so helps to protect the environment.

Private cars pollute the air with poisonous gases. If you use a car to get to school, is it possible to walk or go by bike, bus or train instead? Or can you share the car journey with a family that lives nearby? You could encourage family members to use the car less – or switch to a smaller or more energy-efficient car.

DETECTIVE WORK

How far do you travel by car each week? Ask family members to keep a log of car journeys for a week, and record the mileage. Add up the journeys to work out the total mileage. Could the total be reduced by using public transport for some journeys?

Many city centres now have cycle lanes which make it safer and easier to cycle in traffic.

Your project

If you've done the detective work and answered all of Sherlock's questions, you now know a lot about air pollution and how it can be tackled. Investigate further by making your own project. You could choose from the following ideas.

Practical action

Run a health check on the air in your neighbourhood. Smear a thin layer of petroleum jelly onto two jar lids. Place one indoors and the other outside near the street on a dry day. After a day, check the lids for traces of pollution such as dust and soot. Ask your teacher if you can repeat the experiment inside school and in the grounds.

Topics to investigate

- Investigate air pollution in two different countries. The website listed on page 13 will help you. What are the most serious forms of pollution in each area, and how are they being tackled?
- Find out more about one type of air pollution, such as acid rain, ozone loss or indoor pollution. What is the effect on people and wildlife, and what is being done?
- Find out more about how schools are tackling pollution using this website: www.eco-schools.org.uk/ Ask your teacher if your school can register for this scheme.

Your local library and the Internet can provide all sorts of information. Try the websites listed on page 31. When you have collected the information for your project, you might like to present it in an interesting way, using one of the ideas on page 29.

Planting trees helps to keep the air healthy. Choose a species that grows naturally in your area.

Cycling instead of going by car helps to reduce
air pollution that is caused by vehicles.

Project presentation

- Design a poster to explain all about air pollution and the importance of keeping the air clean.
- Ask your teacher if you can hold a class debate about a particular type of air pollution, such as smoking or acid rain.
- Imagine you are making a television documentary or writing a magazine article about air pollution. Make a plan showing the main points you want to show in the order that makes the most sense.

Sherlock has found out about how climate change is affecting wildlife. Some birds are nesting earlier now springs are warmer. Some animals that usually sleep all winter are spending less time asleep.

Glossary

acid rain Rain that is slightly acidic because of pollution.

atmosphere A layer of gases that surrounds and protects the Earth.

carbon dioxide A gas absorbed by plants and given off by animals as they breathe and by wood, coal and oil when they burn.

catalytic converter A device fitted to a vehicle's exhaust system to reduce air pollution.

chloro-fluorocarbons (CFCs) Chemicals called chloro-fluorocarbons, that have been used in the manufacture of fridges, foam packaging and spray cans, but which damage the ozone layer.

climate change Any long-term significant change in the weather patterns of an area.

conservation Work done to protect the natural world.

drought A long period of dry weather.

emissions Amounts of a gas given off.

environmentally friendly Of a substance that does not harm the natural world.

fossil fuels Fuels that are made of fossilised plants or animals that lived in prehistoric times, for example coal, oil, and natural gas.

fuel A substance that can be burned or used up to produce energy.

generate To produce something.

global warming Rising temperatures worldwide, caused by the increase of gases in the air that trap the Sun's heat near the Earth.

gravity The natural pull of the Earth, Moon or Sun.

Greenhouse Effect The warming effect caused by certain gases in the atmosphere that trap heat rising from Earth's surface.

greenhouse gases Gases in the atmosphere that trap the Sun's heat.

habitat A particular place where plants and animals live, such as a forest or a desert.

hydrogen A gas which produces water when combined with oxygen.

Ice Age A long period when the climate was colder and huge areas of the world were covered in ice.

industrialise When a country develops its industries, so that many factories and power plants are built.

insecticide A chemical sprayed on plants to kill plant-eating pests.

insulate To prevent energy such as heat from escaping and being wasted.

kerosene A fuel used by aircraft.

lichen Living things that grow on stones and tree trunks. Lichens are a combination of a tiny plant and a fungus.

meteor Rocks and dust entering the atmosphere from space.

oxygen A gas that makes up one-fifth of Earth's atmosphere, which animals use to breathe.

ozone layer A layer of ozone gas found in the atmosphere. It reduces the harmful ultraviolet rays in sunlight reaching Earth.

particle A tiny piece of matter, such as an atom or grain of dust.

photochemical smog A dirty haze that forms in the air when sunlight reacts with pollution from factories and car exhausts.

pollution Any substance that harms the natural world.

radioactive Of a material that gives off dangerous radiation.

raw material A natural materials such as a mineral or timber.

recycling When waste materials are used again to make new products.

respiration The process of releasing carbon dioxide by animals and plants.

scrubber A device that can be fitted to a factory chimney to filter out pollution.

smog A poisonous haze caused by pollution.

solar To do with the Sun.

transboundary When something crosses a natural border between countries.

ultraviolet rays Harmful rays in sunlight which can cause health problems for animals and people.

water vapour Moisture in the form of a gas.

Answers

☙ **Page 4:** Aircraft mostly fly in the stratosphere.

☙ **Page 6:** Carbon dioxide is released when animals breathe out, when plants or animals decay, and when fuels such as wood and coal are burned. The oceans can also release carbon dioxide.

☙ **Page 12:** Russia.

☙ **Page 14:** Gas and ash given off by volcanoes also contribute to acid rain.

☙ **Page 18:** VOCs are found in some paints, glues, aerosols and cleaning products.

☙ **Page 22:** When forests burn, smoke pollutes the air and carbon dioxide is released, increasing the Greenhouse Effect. Dead trees no longer absorb carbon dioxide or release oxygen.

☙ **Page 25:** Wind and solar power provide energy without releasing the greenhouse gases that are causing climate change.

Further information

Further reading

The Geography Detecive Investigates: Pollution
by Jen Green (Wayland, 2009)

Improving Our Environment: Air Pollution
by Jen Green (Wayland, 2005)

Protecting Our Planet: Energy in Crisis
by Catherine Chambers (Wayland, 2009)

Websites

Department for Environment, UK
www.defra.gov.uk/environment/climate/index.htm

www.clean-air-kids.org.uk/airquality.html

US government sites on air pollution for students
www.epa.gov/kids/air.htm

www.epa.gov/students/air.html

US government Environmental Kids Club
www.epa.gov/kids/

Conservation organisations

Friends of the Earth
www.foei.org/

Greenpeace
www.greenpeace.org/

World Wildlife Fund (WWF)
www.worldwildlife.org

Environment Protection Authority, Australia
www.environment.gov.au/

The Young People's Trust for the Environment
www.ypte.org.uk/

Environmental Investigation Agency
www.eia-international.org

Index

The Environment Detective Investigates

Contents of titles in the series:

WAYLAND